Jane Austen's family and Tonbridge

Jane Austen, by James Andrews of Maidenhead from an earlier watercolour
by Jane's sister Cassandra. This was produced as a steel engraving for the
frontispiece of the *Memoir of Jane Austen* in 1870 by her nephew
James Edward Austen-Leigh.

MARGARET WILSON

Jane Austen's family and Tonbridge

THE JANE AUSTEN SOCIETY
in association with the Kent Branch

First published in Great Britain 2001
by the Jane Austen Society
c/o Jane Austen's House, Chawton, Alton GU34 1SD

© Copyright 2001 Margaret Wilson

ISBN 0-9538174-0-7

Printed by Sarsen Press, 22 Hyde Street, Winchester, SO23 7DR

Contents

Preface	7
Introduction	9
The early Austens	10
Jane's great-grandmother, Elizabeth Weller – a remarkable woman	14
Elizabeth Weller's children – in need of education	16
Jane's father, George – a handsome man	20
George's cousin, Henry – clergyman of West Kent	24
Jane's Tonbridge aunts – contrasting lives	29
The Austen step relations – the affectionate Walters	31
Phylly Walter – a country cousin	34
The Sevenoaks Austens – pillars of the community	38
Jane Austen and Tonbridge	40
James Stanier Clarke	41
John George Children	42
Vicesimus Knox and Thomas Jefferson – two writers	43
John Papillon	46
Epilogue	48
Bibliography	51
Notes	53
Family Trees	57
Index	59

The Society gratefully acknowledges the generosity of the family of
Alice Chetwynd Ley for the donation of her Public Lending Rights.

This reprint is in loving memory of her and of her husband, Ken Ley,
both admirers of Jane Austen's writing and her wit.

Preface

In September 2000 a plaque was unveiled at Tonbridge School to commemorate Jane Austen's father George, who was both pupil and teacher there. It seems appropriate to follow this event with a publication about the Austen family and their many connections with Tonbridge and its surrounding area. At the invitation of the Jane Austen Society I have undertaken this task, incorporating recent research and the work of local historians. For some time the pamphlet by Sylvia Andrews was the only published work on the subject, and hard to find. More recently, the research work of Gilbert Hoole has provided invaluable information. His *Tonbridge Miscellany*, together with his research notes lodged with Tonbridge School Library and Tonbridge Public Library, have formed the core of this booklet. I pay tribute to his meticulous scholarship over many years. The work of Sir David Waldron Smithers in a broader Kentish context has also been most useful. I hope that by drawing together all that is known of the Austens in Tonbridge and its environs I am providing something that will be of interest both to local readers and others wishing to know more of the novelist's family background.

I am grateful to the following for their invaluable assistance in the preparation and production of this booklet: Alwyn Austen, Tom Carpenter, David Gilson, Deirdre Le Faye, Helen Lefroy, Chris Viveash, Anthony Wilson and the Staff of Tonbridge School Library.

I owe a particular debt to Bunty Goldup, whose perceptive comments on my text were just one aspect of her energetic support for the Kent Branch of the Jane Austen Society, but who sadly did not live to see the book published.

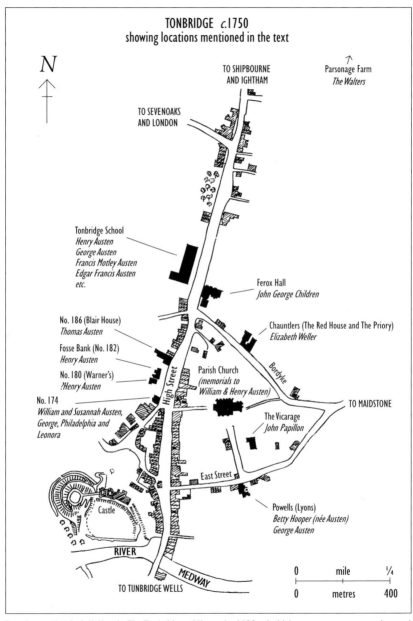

TONBRIDGE c.1750
showing locations mentioned in the text

N

TO SHIPBOURNE
AND IGHTHAM

Parsonage Farm
The Walters

TO SEVENOAKS
AND LONDON

Tonbridge School
Henry Austen
George Austen
Francis Motley Austen
Edgar Francis Austen
etc.

Ferox Hall
John George Children

No. 186 (Blair House)
Thomas Austen

Chauntlers (The Red House and The Priory)
Elizabeth Weller

Fosse Bank (No. 182)
Henry Austen

No. 180 (Warner's)
?Henry Austen

Parish Church
(memorials to
William & Henry Austen)

High Street

Bordyke

TO MAIDSTONE

No. 174
William and Susannah Austen,
George, Philadelphia and
Leonora

The Vicarage
John Papillon

East Street

Castle

Powells (Lyons)
Betty Hooper (née Austen)
George Austen

RIVER

MEDWAY

TO TUNBRIDGE WELLS

| 0 | mile | ¼ |
| 0 | metres | 400 |

Based on a plan in A. H. Neve's *The Tonbridge of Yesterday*, 1933, of which some aspects are conjectural.

8

Introduction

In the opening chapter of *Persuasion* Jane Austen portrays the gloriously vain character Sir Walter Elliot perusing with smug satisfaction his own family's entry in the Baronetage, describing 'The history and rise of the ancient and respectable family in the usual terms'. The Austens, Jane's paternal forebears, were also an ancient and respectable family but, as gentry, would not have featured in any such volume; nor, unlike Sir Walter, would Jane have revelled in their status if they had. The Austens had deep roots in Kent. Jane was born and brought up in Hampshire, but the West Kent link was formative in her family's history and continued to impinge upon the lives of family members, both in her lifetime and beyond.

Jane herself may well have visited Tonbridge but there is no surviving record of such a visit. However, we know that she came to nearby Sevenoaks in 1788, when she and her parents stayed with her wealthy great-uncle Francis in The Red House, which can still be seen in the High Street, floodlit in the evenings to emphasise its Georgian elegance. As was typical of the time, many of the Austens had large families, and there were several second marriages and marriages within the extended family. Disentangling them all requires a clear head but the family trees on pages 57-8 may help. Fifty-one members of the Austen clan are mentioned in this booklet, of whom twenty-two lived in Tonbridge, at least for part of their lives, twenty-one lived within a few miles of the town, eight were educated at Tonbridge School and seven have memorials in the parish church.

Tonbridge was also home to several people whom Jane knew or mentioned in her letters. An old boy of Tonbridge School, James Stanier Clarke, was the link between Jane and the Prince Regent, to whom in 1815 she dedicated *Emma*. Opposite Tonbridge School lived John George Children of Ferox Hall, who is mentioned in one of Jane's letters and was a distant relation. The vicar of Tonbridge, John Papillon, later became her parish priest in Chawton, the Hampshire village where Jane lived at the end of her life. All in all the Tonbridge connection is a strong one.

Tonbridge itself in the mid eighteenth century was a town of some two thousand people; medieval in origin, it clustered round its castle, church and river crossing. But it is important to remember that this growing town stood amid hopgardens and orchards in a county which, as Jane's cousin Eliza wrote, contained 'shade and pure air' much preferable to the 'smoke and dirt' of London.[1] The parish was the largest in Kent, extending southwards to include the developing spa of Tunbridge Wells, soon to become a separate and much better known entity. As a thriving market town, Tonbridge was a centre that served the needs of a network of outlying villages, in one of which, Horsmonden, the earliest records of the Austens are found.

The early Austens

On the floor of the nave of Horsmonden church there is a memorial tablet containing a worn shield bearing the Austen arms. This heraldic device was allowed to two Astyns, of Chevening and Yalding, in the late sixteenth century and they were very probably Jane's ancestors. The first Austen whom we can name with any certainty as an ancestor was John who lived from c.1560 to 1620, six generations before the novelist. For convenience he is usually known as John Austen I. His family lived in the Goudhurst and Horsmonden area in the heart of the Kentish Weald. (The West Kent map on page 33 shows the location of villages and towns in the area.) It was probably at this time that the Austens acquired the Tudor manor house of Broadford, which still stands a mile from the village centre in Horsmonden.[1] They were a family belonging to the community of clothmakers who had established themselves around Cranbrook in the late sixteenth century and whose reputation had earned them the title of 'Grey Coats of

Kent' after their plain dress. Jane Austen may have been aware of her family's Kentish ancestry for there is a handwritten note, possibly by Jane or her father, in Jane's copy of Richard Warner's *Excursions from Bath* (1801). Below a reference to woollen works at Wootton-under-Edge belonging 'to Messrs. Austin' is written: 'A branch of the Austens – the "Gray Coats of Kent"'.[2]

Grovehurst, a Wealden hall-house in Horsmonden, home of Jane's ancestors in the seventeenth century.

John I and his wife Joan are buried in Horsmonden church. Joan died in 1604 and is commemorated by a brass effigy showing her dressed in Jacobean costume. Her life was brought abruptly to a close when, after bearing seven children, she died giving birth to twins. The wording on her memorial bears witness to a deep personal faith: 'let neither hvsband nor children nor lands nor goods separate me from the my God'. Their son Francis I expanded the family possessions by acquiring another manor house, Grovehurst.[3] This gabled house still stands on a hill to the east of the village. Rather smaller than Broadford, it is a good example of a Wealden hall-house. Francis's

Horsmonden Church, where Jane's ancestors are buried.

son, John III, therefore inherited a substantial legacy and after marrying Jane Atkins, had a family of two sons and three daughters. The marriages of his daughters are recorded on the same memorial tablet in Horsmonden church as that which bears the Austen arms, worn almost invisible by the feet of parishioners over the years. One of these marriages is particularly significant for a study of the family fortunes. A daughter called Jane (by now a family name) married Stephen Stringer of Goudhurst and it is their grand-daughter, also Jane, who married Thomas Brodnax of Godmersham, near Canterbury, later known as Thomas Knight and owner also of two Hampshire estates, Steventon and Chawton. Godmersham and Chawton both figured prominently in the life of the novelist through the inheritance of them by her brother Edward. Jane made frequent visits to Edward and his family at Godmersham Park and it was Edward who provided Chawton Cottage as a home for his widowed mother, Jane and her sister Cassandra.

The heir of John Austen III, John IV, should have been confident of a secure future for his family but events and his character were ultimately to deny him this. He married Elizabeth Weller on 29 December 1693 and it is her entry into the family history that marks the first direct link between the Austens and Tonbridge, for she came from a Tonbridge family, several generations of whom are commemorated in the parish church. The Wellers lived in Chauntlers, a substantial house with ancient origins, in Bordyke. It had been acquired in c.1631 by Elizabeth's grandfather Thomas, who played an important role in local events in the Civil War. It later passed to Elizabeth's brother, Robert, and remained in the family for several generations. Chauntlers has since been divided into two properties, now known as The Priory and The Red House.

Chauntlers (now The Priory and The Red House) in Bordyke, Tonbridge, where Jane's great-grandmother Elizabeth Weller lived before her marriage.

Elizabeth Weller was brought up at Chauntlers but moved to the Austen home at Broadford on her marriage. An inventory of 1708 which has survived in family papers shows what sort of house she

13

was in charge of. It was clearly a comfortable residence with rooms ranging from parlour, hall, little parlour, and several chambers (bedrooms) to brewhouse, bakehouse, milkhouse, and stable. Oak panelling in a large room on the first floor and carvings of the Tudor rose and the Austen arms over the fireplace all go to show the prosperity of the family at this date. The couple's family expanded rapidly; by 1704 Elizabeth had given birth to one daughter and six sons. But in the same year John Austen IV died unexpectedly of tuberculosis.

Jane's great-grandmother, Elizabeth Weller – a remarkable woman

The story of how Elizabeth Weller dealt with her misfortune and brought up seven children is an uplifting tale of a strong character's victory over adversity, all the more remarkable for her being a woman. Her determination is one of the most admirable characteristics to be found in the Austen lineage and some like to detect this trait in her famous great-grand-daughter. Speculation apart, it is certainly true that Jane's grandfather, William, would never have had the good start in life which his mother gave him, if Elizabeth had succumbed to self-pity at the daunting prospect before her.

We are fortunately able to get a good picture of how she solved her difficulties from a surviving manuscript of 1706-8, known as her Memorandum. Elizabeth's most obvious problem arose from the unexpectedness of her husband's death. This was compounded by his substantial debts, of which she was hitherto unaware. Elizabeth freely admitted she 'was ever uneasy to be in debt' which made her husband 'keep his debts ye more private, and also was not willing his Father shou'd know of ym [them] fearing his displeasure'.[1] The secrecy which John IV had maintained about his debts made the discovery of them all the more of a shock. Nor did the large size of the family help their situation, for any inheritance divided among so many would be small and would leave the daughter, Betty, with no hope of a substantial dowry with which to attract a husband. Elizabeth had also to contend with a disagreeable trait in the character of her father-in-law, his meanness. He was, as she put it, 'loath to part with anything'.

The old man's general obstructiveness towards his son's widow is evident at every stage of the ensuing proceedings. Elizabeth felt that mourning clothes were required – she was 'loath to appear ridiculous' – and it was only with the assistance of her brothers-in-law, Stephen Stringer and John Holman (the executors), that she was able to extract a mere £10 towards the costs from John III. John IV had been an only son and on his deathbed had been reassured by his father that the latter would provide for the seven children. This promise was soon forgotten and after the 'intreaty of many friends' Elizabeth even considered selling her 'household goods'. Fortunately John III stopped the sale, but haggling between the two continued until, in July 1705, he was taken suddenly ill and died.

This second death led to further difficulties, for his will was characteristically unfair and made Elizabeth 'appear as no friend nay rather an enemy to ye Family'. Only her eldest son, John, would be comfortably off; his education and future alone were provided for, a fact which mystified his mother: 'why my Father Austen shou'd endeavour so much for my eldest son, more than my other children I can't well tell.' Elizabeth's account book for this period gives detailed evidence of her continual efforts to make ends meet. She eventually managed to pay off her husband's debts by the sale of some of her effects (including her silver plate) and by stringent economies.

In 1708, when her eldest son was twelve and educational needs had become a priority, Elizabeth decided that the family should move from Broadford. She therefore took a post as housekeeper to the headmaster of Sevenoaks School, which she considered to be 'very proper for my circumstances', for while looking after other boarders at the school she would get her own children's education free. 'I cou'd not do a better thing for my Children's good, their education being my great care . . . I always tho't if they had Learning, they might ye better shift in ye world.' In this respect her outlook about the importance of education was similar to that of Jane Austen's parents.

The question of why Elizabeth chose Sevenoaks instead of Tonbridge School is worth considering. Neither school was enjoying a prosperous phase at this time, so that would not have been a factor in her choice. It is more likely to have been for another reason: the headmaster of Tonbridge School was married so had no need of a housekeeper, whereas Elijah Fenton, the head of Sevenoaks, was a bachelor. 'I take God to witness' she wrote, 'that my removing to Sen'nock was in hopes to make it for my Children's benefitt'. Nor was she disappointed. Her accounts for the years 1708-19 give us an idea of how carefully she budgeted for her children's needs, with expenses for books, wax candles, clothes and pocket money increasing over the years. Illness brought more expenditure, particularly in 1715-16, with £11 4s. 6d. being paid for 'physick' and Frank specifically mentioned as having smallpox the previous year. Only determination and careful economy enabled this single parent to make a success of her children's upbringing.

Elizabeth Weller's children – in need of education

Elizabeth's eldest child, Elizabeth known as Betty, was probably educated at home. By the time she was nineteen the expenditure on her clothes (an important feature in attracting a husband) had risen to £8 17s. and nearly double that in the following year. Luckily she was successful in the marriage market for she married one of the Hooper family, almost certainly George (born in 1691) an attorney, the fifth generation of a Tonbridge law firm founded in the sixteenth century by Nicholas Hooper.[1] Their house was called Powells (now known as Lyons) in East Street. (The location of Powells and other buildings can be found on the map of Tonbridge on page 8.)

Of the six boys, the oldest, John (whom I shall call John Austen V) was the only one Elizabeth did not have to support from her own means, and I shall deal with him later. Francis II, the next eldest, was six when his father died. After his education at Sevenoaks he was apprenticed in 1714 to an attorney, George Tilden, in Bedford Row,

London for £140.[2] When he had qualified he returned to Sevenoaks and practised most successfully as a solicitor. With two marriages and three sons, he became an important person in the family history and is known to have met the novelist herself. Interestingly, the sum spent on his training was the highest of all the brothers and he also became the most prosperous. Thomas, next in age, was at first destined for a career in trade, and went from Sevenoaks School to be apprenticed for £60 to a London haberdasher, Henry Wells, in November 1715.[3] He later reappeared in Tonbridge as an apothecary, married Elizabeth Burgess and had a son Henry who features later in the family story. They lived in a house of medieval origin, now No. 186 at the north end of the High Street (known over the years as The Star and The White Horse Inn). It has recently been restored as offices, Blair House. Thomas ended his days in Tonbridge and is buried there, although no memorial to him can now be found in the church or churchyard.

With the fourth son, William, we come to the most significant of Elizabeth's offspring, for he was Jane's grandfather. Born on 3 February 1701, he was a mere three years old when his father died. After his Sevenoaks education he was apprenticed at the age of seventeen to William Ellis, a Woolwich surgeon, for the sum of £115 10s.[4] He returned to practise in Tonbridge, and c.1727 he married Rebecca, daughter of a Gloucester physician Sir George Hampson, and widow of William Walter, about whom more later.

Rebecca already had a son from her first marriage; she and William Austen proceeded to have their own family of four children. The eldest, a daughter called Hampson, died before the age of two in 1730. Another daughter, Philadelphia, was born in that year and the all-important George in 1731, with the last daughter Leonora arriving in 1732. Rebecca herself died in February of that year, soon after Leonora's birth, and for four years the children were motherless. Their father remarried on 30 May 1736 a Susannah Kelk, thirteen years his senior, and enjoyed a brief second marriage, which terminated in his death on 7 December 1737.

The social position in Tonbridge of Jane's grandfather is a matter of some interest. The status of apothecaries or surgeons at this time was not an elevated one. Early in the following century Jane Austen

17

Tonbridge Parish Church in 1857, from *Tonbridge Legends, etc.*, anon.,
published by Richard Ware, Tonbridge, n.d..

The grave of Jane's grandfather, William Austen, in Tonbridge Parish Church.
© *Tonbridge Parish Church*

showed that they were not counted among other professions or the gentry. In a letter to her niece Anna Lefroy on 10 August 1814, her view on a fictional character's contact with nobility is that a 'Country Surgeon would not be introduced to Men of their rank'.[5] However, although socialising may have been restricted for a surgeon, he could still be a man of some standing in the community, and William Austen would have been respected in Tonbridge.

The question of where William Austen lived in the town is not easily answered. Gilbert Hoole has examined the marriage settlement, dated 29 April 1736, of William and his second wife, which conveyed 'the messuage, formerly The Greyhound, afterwards The Bell, . . . now a private house in possession of William Austen lying on the West side of the Town, with piece of land adjacent.'[6] When William Austen died the following year Susannah inherited all her husband's property and when she herself died in 1768, the house was sold to Thomas Slatter of Tonbridge, also a surgeon. This fact identifies the site, for in 1780 T. Slatter is known to have lived at what is now No. 174 High Street. This property was, until a fire in 1997, the furnishing shop of Paul Bonner, where the structure of the old house could be discerned within the building. It is now a charred ruin, awaiting rebuilding.

William Austen and his family are well recorded in the Parish Church, where there is a memorial to them on the floor of the north aisle. This is not normally accessible, but a photograph of part of it is displayed nearby.

Elizabeth's two remaining sons were Robert and Stephen. Robert left home when he was sixteen after which little is known about him, except that he died of smallpox, unmarried, at the age of only twenty-six and is buried at Tenterden. His brother Stephen had only just been born when his father died. After schooling at Sevenoaks he was apprenticed in 1719 to a London stationer, William Innys, for £105 and became a bookseller in St Paul's Churchyard. He married, had one son and died aged forty-seven. Appropriately he is buried in the village of the family's roots, Horsmonden.

This leaves the career of the eldest son, John V. Treated differently by his grandfather, who according to Elizabeth, tended to have 'always a particular favorite child', he was the main beneficiary of the family inheritance. The place of his early schooling is unknown; his uncles Stringer and Holman wanted him to go somewhere other than Sevenoaks but unfortunately Tonbridge School (the obvious alternative) has no school lists for the years 1707-11 so we cannot be sure that he went there. The appearance of John's name on a subscription list to the school library fund in 1724/5 suggests he may have had some link with the school, but more than that is speculation. We do know that in 1713 he went up to Pembroke College, Cambridge. Later he took over the family home at Broadford and married his cousin, Mary Stringer, by whom he had three children, John VI, Jane and Elizabeth. After an unremarkable and short life, he died at the age of thirty-two and is buried at Horsmonden. As a postscript to this branch of Jane's family, it is worth mentioning the novelist's comment when John VI died without heir in 1807. There was general family interest in the fate of Broadford and Jane wrote, somewhat peevishly: 'It is believed at Tunbridge that he has left everything after the death of his widow to Mr My [Motley] Austen's third son John . . . Such ill-gotten Wealth can never prosper!'.[7] Francis Motley Austen was the eldest son of Francis II, the Sevenoaks solicitor. To discover that an already wealthy branch of the family was to be further enriched by the acquisition of the ancestral home must have been galling.

Elizabeth herself lived for only two years after her youngest son left school but she died secure in the knowledge that she had given her children a good start in life. She is buried at Tonbridge, although sadly no memorial to this remarkable woman can now be found in the church or churchyard.

Jane's father, George – a handsome man

Elizabeth Weller's belief in the importance of a good education for her children was the guiding force during her widowhood. Her great-grand-daughter, Jane, in *Persuasion*, shows that she too recognised how fortunate men – as opposed to women – are in receiving sound teaching. Anne Eliot says as much to Captain Harville: 'Men have had every advantage of us in telling their own story. Education has been theirs in so much higher a degree.'[1]

Jane's father, George, received an excellent education, not at Sevenoaks but at Tonbridge School. But he was quite lucky to do so, since he had been orphaned at an early age. Fortunately for him, there were generous relatives on hand to help. When his father died in 1737, his stepmother, Susannah, had no legal obligation to support her stepchildren since her husband had not updated his will. She showed no interest in them, and their care devolved upon other members of the family. At first their uncle Stephen, the London bookseller, took them on but according to a manuscript family history he was unsympathetic and George was soon sent to live in Tonbridge with his aunt Betty Hooper at her home in East Street.[2] From the age of ten he attended Tonbridge School, thanks to the generosity of his uncle Francis, the rich attorney in Sevenoaks, who paid the fees. Here George gained a thorough education which established a sound intellectual foundation for the rest of his life.

Tonbridge School in the eighteenth century was not a major public school, but a grammar school, founded two centuries earlier for the boys of the town and adjacent country. The school occupied a stone building, set a little back from the High Street (now London Road) but running parallel with it, extending south from what is now the Cawthorn Lecture Theatre. The school building had a high pitched roof, with dormer windows and a central cupola containing the school bell. At the south end was a tall decorative chimney which had a sundial on one side. At this end were the Master's quarters while those of the Usher (or Assistant Master) were at the north end. Unfortunately nothing substantial remains of this building.

The school's founding charter decreed that local boys who could read and write some English and Latin and could pay sixpence a year were entitled to an education at the school. These boys, known as Foundationers, made up a small number of the total, and in George Austen's time there were only 9 out of a total of 62 pupils. Most of the boys were boarders who lived in the school; the pupils came mainly from the gentry, some were titled, some came from London and some from the West Indies. The age at which a boy entered the school varied considerably; George Austen came at ten, his cousins Henry and Francis Motley at eight and Henry's son Edgar at nine.

The school day was a strenuous one; lessons started at seven in the morning after prayers and lasted until five in the evening, with a break in the middle of the day and more prayers at the end. The importance of religion is also seen in the corporate visit to the Parish Church every Sunday. All the boys were taught in the same 40 foot-long room with a high ceiling, lit by diamond-paned windows; the headmaster taught several groups at one end of the room, while the Usher (the post later held by George) taught groups at the other end. It must have been a noisy environment with only the most motivated gaining much benefit.

Before entering the school, boys had to be able to read and write both Latin and English. The education was almost exclusively in the Classics, i.e. Latin and Greek, and the masters would frequently speak Latin to those boys who could understand it well. Latin was all-important for those intending to enter the Law and the Church (as George did), while French, arithmetic and writing were taught as extras for a fee.

The fluctuation in the numbers of the school depended much upon the Headmaster. When George arrived in 1741 this was the Revd Richard Spencer, who had held the post since 1714, increasing the roll from 32 to 80 within a decade. Two years later he resigned and was replaced by the Revd James Cawthorn, a Yorkshireman of only twenty-four. The combination of his extreme youth and northern origins may have aroused suspicion among the Tonbridge population; whatever the cause, the numbers dropped dramatically. Cawthorn was known as a strict disciplinarian and his reputation for severity contrasts strongly with his passion for music and poetry. His influence on George must have been considerable, for he was his teacher and later his colleague. Moreover, his opinion of George must have been good, for he chose him for the position of Usher, a job in which he would work at very close quarters with him, requiring trust and respect on the part of both men. Some years later an anthology of Cawthorn's verse was published by public subscription and although George's name does not appear (by that time he was living in Hampshire and out of touch) another family name, that of John Austen V of Broadford, does. A memorial to Cawthorn (with Latin epitaph) can be seen in Tonbridge Parish Church.

There is no doubt that George flourished as a pupil at the school, for his name appears high in the class order. In 1747 when he was due to leave, the Sir Thomas White fellowship at St John's College Oxford, reserved for a boy from Tonbridge, fell vacant and was awarded to George. This would provide long-term financial support as a cleric until the time of his marriage. In 1751 he received his B A and two years later won a Smythe Exhibition from the school, for which his status as an orphan entitled him to apply. A combination of his circumstances and talent had thus enabled him to continue his education and pursue his vocation as a teacher and churchman.

In 1754 he was ordained deacon at Oxford and in that year took up the post of Usher, or Second Master, at his old school, together

Tonbridge School as it was from 1760 to 1825, from W. G. Hart's
Register of Tonbridge School 1553-1820. Tonbridge School Library

with a perpetual curacy at Shipbourne, a village three miles north of Tonbridge. The latter had previously been held by his cousin Henry, who had moved on to the Knight family living of Steventon in Hampshire. A year later George was ordained priest at Rochester and continued to work in the Tonbridge area for another two years. His Oxford college allowed absence for up to five years and he retained links by living in his college rooms during the school's summer holidays. School records show that he left his post as Usher in March 1757 and Shipbourne parish records indicate that he ceased to function as curate in the same year.

George was recalled to Oxford to be assistant chaplain of his College and pursued his theological studies there, holding the additional post of Junior Proctor (1759-60). During this period he was given the nickname of 'the handsome proctor', and his responsibilities in the role were considerable, for besides ceremonial and administrative duties, he had to police the streets at night, and also exercise political skill in organising support when university statutes required change – a task he did with great effect.[3]

George finally left Oxford in 1761 when he succeeded to the living of Steventon in Hampshire, again following his cousin Henry. There he spent the rest of his career, retiring in 1801, this part of his life being well chronicled in biographies of his daughter. In 1764 he married Cassandra Leigh, with whom he brought up eight children, of whom Jane was the seventh. Scholarly and mild, industrious and fair, George Austen was the epitome of a man happy in his family and his job, whose children enjoyed huge benefits from the stable and caring environment he and his wife engendered.

George Austen's cousin, Henry – clergyman of West Kent

George was not the only Austen to attend Tonbridge School. His cousin Henry and Henry's son Edgar, his half-brother William Hampson Walter (the son of his mother's first marriage), and Francis Motley (son of Uncle Francis) were all pupils. The latter appears in the School Register for only one year, 1755, when he may have been taught by George; he was then only eight so must have gone elsewhere or possibly had tutors for the rest of his education. He later went up to Hertford College, Oxford, after which he lived the life of a gentleman of leisure in Sevenoaks.

George's cousin Henry, the son of Thomas Austen the Tonbridge apothecary, was five years older than George and reached the top of the school, becoming head boy when George was in his second year. The two cousins must certainly have known each other. Henry was an able boy and went on to Queen's College, Cambridge, where he held a Smythe Exhibition. Destined for the Church, he was ordained deacon at Rochester in 1747 at the early age of twenty-one, two years under the canonical age, so needing a dispensation from the Archbishop. He was perpetual curate at Shipbourne until 1754 when George took over. In that year Henry was appointed curate of Chiddingstone, a village to the west of Tonbridge, and in 1759 he succeeded to the living of Steventon in Hampshire (which was within family patronage), where he remained until 1761 when he was again followed by his cousin George. Henry then moved to another family living, West Wickham, where he stayed a further nineteen years.

Amidst all these changes Henry did not in actual fact move as much as one would expect. He does not seem to have lived in Hampshire, preferring to use a curate there. He was an energetic personality, however, and is known to have performed duties conscientiously at Chiddingstone, which is a manageable journey from Tonbridge. Parish records show that he signed every marriage certificate there from February 1755 to December 1762 (and some in April 1753),[1] so he cannot have been a casual minister. At West Wickham, too, he performed many duties and it was here that his five children were baptised and one is buried, according to Gilbert Hoole who has studied the parish records. Henry's later life is not without some controversy, for it is claimed that while at West Wickham he developed Unitarian views [2] and despite the efforts of the Archbishop to dissuade him, he resigned his living and returned to Tonbridge. However, his memorial, which is on the north wall of the parish church, shows that the Church still allowed him to use the title Reverend.

Fosse Bank, the home of George Austen's cousin Henry, as it was in the mid-nineteenth century. *Tonbridge Historical Society*

Although we have no direct evidence as to where Henry resided during the years before he moved to West Wickham , it seems likely that he remained in his father's home at 186 Tonbridge High Street. He certainly kept up his social contact in the town, for in 1763 he married Mary Hooker, of a well known local family who owned Tonbridge Castle. By her he had five children of whom three, Elizabeth Matilda, Harriet and Edgar, survived infancy. On his return to the town in 1780, Henry moved, according to Hoole, into a house called Fosse Bank, which his brother-in-law Thomas Hooker had just vacated, next door to Henry's old childhood home in the High Street. Fosse Bank – a place of Georgian elegance, with coach house and stables – later became the Tonbridge Ladies College, intended as a school for the sisters of boys attending Tonbridge School. It has now been replaced by an office block, No. 182. Henry may then have moved to the adjoining house which is now offices of the solicitors Warner's at No. 180.

We cannot be sure if Henry ever met the novelist Jane but we do know that her parents visited the family in 1783. The occasion was later recalled by their son Frank, who accompanied them. Nine- year-old Edgar (Henry's son) asked him if he 'knew what "wiring" was, and on my professing ignorance, he very deliberately ran a pin a considerable way into my leg, for which his sister Harriet gave him a scolding. He was at that time a day scholar at Tonbridge School, and therefore was only at home with intervals between school hours so that I had not much opportunity of being enlightened by his practical jokes.'[3] Edgar stayed at Tonbridge School for four years and had some musical ability, for a description survives of him performing a duet with his cousin, Anne Woodgate. He did not go to university and was not very robust; he was described in 1801 as 'very much withered and looks extremely ill'.[4] Edgar and his wife were never prosperous and he died at the early age of twenty-nine.

With Edgar's sister Elizabeth Matilda we are on firmer ground for information, for she had links with Hampshire and knew Jane well. In 1789 Elizabeth Matilda was married at Chawton to the prosperous John Butler Harrison of Southampton. According to a family history she 'was one of the most beautiful women in Kent, & on her way to Chawton to be married, her carriage was escorted as far as the boundaries of Kent by the young men of the county on horseback'.[5] She settled into married life in Southampton, where her husband became mayor, and Jane became godmother to her daughter born in 1793 and named after her mother. The two families became even closer when Jane, her sister and mother came to live in that city from 1806 to 1809. Jane records in January 1809 how she danced at a Ball with Elizabeth Matilda's eldest son, aged nineteen.[6] The lady's beauty is said not to have lasted, for Frances Allnutt (a Woodgate relative) in 1801 wrote 'I saw Mrs Harrison on Friday . . ., never was more shock'd in my life, she really looks quite starved, and has not the remains of a pretty Woman.'[7] However a later engraving of Elizabeth Matilda shows a woman of unremarkable appearance.

Harriet, third child of cousin Henry, is mentioned by Maria Woodgate in January 1796 as 'the fair Circassian' suggesting she was attractive and took part in theatricals which were popular among this social circle.[8] However, she did not marry but stayed at home with her father until he died in 1807. Sarah Woodgate commented on 30 July 1807 that 'Poor Mr Austen was buryed on Wednesday, . . . I am

Elizabeth Matilda Butler Harrison, Jane's second cousin and daughter of
her father's cousin, Henry. She lived at Fosse Bank from 1781 to 1789.
Tonbridge Historical Society

afraid we shall soon lose Miss Austen for a neighbour which we are
extremely sorry for.'[9] Harriet did indeed move on, going to live with
her sister in Southampton, where she too must have known the Austen
ladies. Henry, his wife and two of his sons are commemorated in a
memorial on the north wall of Tonbridge Parish Church.

Jane's Tonbridge aunts – contrasting lives

George Austen's sisters, Philadelphia and Leonora, were both born in Tonbridge but could hardly have lived more different lives. The story of the younger of them, Leonora, was largely a mystery until recently, when research by Deirdre Le Faye has thrown light on her circumstances.[1] Previously all we had was a single letter written in 1770 by Leonora's brother-in-law Tysoe Hancock implying that she may have been companion to a Mrs Hinton. The general silence about her in a family whose members were normally close and communicative suggests that she may have had some physical or mental difficulty. She was born in Tonbridge on 25 January 1732, her mother dying a fortnight later. Her father's death when she was only four left her and her siblings dependent upon the goodwill of other relatives. Leonora remained with her uncle Stephen after her brother George went back to Tonbridge and her sister Philadelphia went to live with cousins on the Hampson side of the family. After Stephen died in 1750, Leonora was cared for by his widow. When the latter remarried another bookseller, John Hinton, Leonora remained with them and over the next thirty-three years lodged with them and a succession of their relatives, maintained throughout by money from her brother and sister, as their bank accounts show. These circumstances and the lack of anything written by Leonora herself leads one to conclude that she may have had a disability and was dependent upon the care of others.

Jane's aunt Philadelphia, Leonora's older sister, was very different. She was baptised in Tonbridge on 15 May 1730 and brought up by maternal relations, the Freemans (her mother's sister Catherine having married a John Freeman). A recent discovery by Robin Vick of her name in the apprentice register in May 1745 indicates that at fifteen she began an apprenticeship to a Covent Garden milliner.[2] However her natural spirit and ambition led her to leave for India in 1750. A pretty and lively girl, she soon found a husband, Tysoe Hancock. He was a surgeon with the East India Company and seven years her senior. They married in 1753 and had a single child, Eliza, a cousin of Jane Austen who would eventually marry Jane's brother Henry.

Eliza's godfather was the famed Warren Hastings, a friend of her father who would be important in helping with family finances later. When Eliza was four the family returned to England, but after Tysoe's business interests failed to flourish he went back to India where he died in 1775. In England Philadelphia and her daughter resumed contact with their relatives, paying visits to the George Austen branch in Steventon, and to their step relations, the Walters, near Tonbridge, one of whom later wrote of her aunt Hancock in glowing terms: 'I do not know a fault she has – so strictly just and honourable in all her dealings, so kind and obliging to all her friends and acquaintance, so religious in all her actions, in short I do not know a person that has more the appearance of perfection.'[3]

Left: Jane's aunt, Philadelphia Hancock, in a miniature by John Smart c.1768. *Jane Austen Memorial Trust.* Right: her brother George Austen, Jane's father. The silhouette, belonging to Tonbridge School, is similar to one at the Jane Austen Museum, Chawton. *Tonbridge School, by permission of the Headmaster*

In 1777 Philadelphia Hancock and her daughter (helped by Hastings' money) went to live on the Continent and eventually settled in Paris where the spirited Eliza sampled fashionable life and acquired her first husband, the young Jean François Capot de Feuillide. When she became pregnant, Eliza returned to England with her mother for the birth of her son Hastings in June 1786. Her mother died in London of breast cancer in 1791 and her husband who was still in France was guillotined three years later. Eliza later remarried, her second husband being Jane Austen's brother Henry.

The importance of Jane's Hancock aunt and cousin in the family history may go further than being mere relations who kept in touch. It has been suggested that their characters influenced Jane's imagination and that Mrs Dashwood in *Sense and Sensibility* owed something to Aunt Philadelphia[4] and that some of Eliza's vivacity can be detected in the lively females of other novels. Whether true or not, it is clear that Jane appreciated the contact she had with this branch of her family and the wider horizons they reflected.

The Austen step relations – the affectionate Walters

Jane's grandmother, Rebecca, married twice and her first husband's family, the Walters, were Tonbridge based. Although only step relations of the Austens, they are important in the family story, as they continued to keep in close touch with Jane's parents. Rebecca was the daughter of Sir George Hampson, a physician of Gloucester, who had inherited a baronetcy in 1719. Her first husband was William Walter who may have come from Tonbridge, where the name of Walter was common in the Trench area to the north of the town. He may be the William Walter who attended Tonbridge School from 1706 to 1714 and was buried in Gloucester as a 'Doctor of Fisick' in 1726.[1] He left Rebecca with a five-year-old son, William Hampson Walter, and it seems likely that at this point Rebecca and the boy came to Tonbridge. It was here that she met William Austen whom she married in the following year and by whom she had her second family, which included Jane's father, George.

Jane Austen's depiction of step-children in *Sense and Sensibility*, where John Dashwood is materially better off than his half-sisters Eleanor and Marianne, does not portray a close bond between them.

But in Jane's real family there was warm affection between her father and his half-brother William Hampson Walter, only ten years his senior. Like George Austen, William Hampson was a pupil at Tonbridge School from 1730 to 1734 but, unlike his half-brother, he did not enter a profession. He married Susannah Weaver of Maidstone in about 1745 and although they lived in Tonbridge parish, all of their seven children, born between 1747 and 1761, were baptised (and two were buried) in Shipbourne church. This was the place where cousin Henry Austen and George Austen held the post of curate during those years. The correspondence between the two branches of the family which has survived has the advantage of telling us where the Walters lived. They dwelt for a time in Upper Trench, a house situated to the north of the town and convenient for Shipbourne.

Never very well off, the Walters led an unexceptionable life but remained friendly with George Austen and his wife and thus enabled the latter to retain a link with West Kent. From 1770 to 1775 their address was 'The Parsonage, near Tunbridge' which Gilbert Hoole identifies almost certainly as Parsonage Farm on the site later occupied by Yardley Court preparatory school, now itself demolished.[2] There is a suggestion in a letter from Jane's mother, Cassandra Austen, to Susannah Walter that the Walters were not entirely happy in this house.[3] Mrs Walter and her daughter kept up contact by going to visit the Austens in Steventon while Mr Walter was away and the two women continued to correspond, exchanging news of their families in an affectionate manner. In July 1771 Mrs George Austen, having just given birth to Henry, wrote to her 'Dear Sister Walter' with the news and enquired if 'my Bror. Walter is got quite well of that complaint in his Leg you mention'd' and hoping it would not prevent a visit from them she wrote 'perhaps he will travail in his Chair, and then perhaps my Dear Sister will accompany him, I am sure I need not say how happy you would make us. I wish we were not so many Miles apart.'[4] By 1780 the Walters, who seem to have been permanently restless, had moved again, this time to Ightham, a village five miles north of Tonbridge, where they appear to have been more content, according to a letter from Eliza de Feuillide to her cousin Phylly Walter.[5] By 1785 the Walters made their last move, this time to Seal, a village between Ightham and Sevenoaks. It was here that William Hampson died in April 1798.

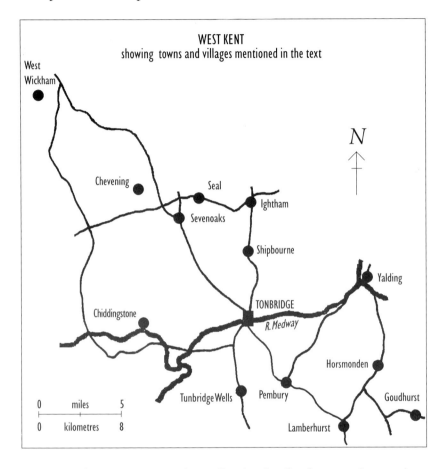

Of the five surviving Walter offspring by far the most interesting, from the Austen point of view, are the youngest James and Philadelphia, known as Phylly. James Walter was George Austen's godson and attended Tonbridge School before going to Corpus Christi College, Cambridge, as a Smythe Exhibitioner like his godfather. Eliza de Feuillide later recalled how James who was one year older than her, had been a young admirer. In a letter to his sister Phylly in 1782 she wrote: ' . . . he made verses on me in which he compared me to

Venus and I know not what other Divinity, and played off fireworks in the cellar in honour of my charms. This happened as you may recollect in a visit I paid to Tonbridge some years ago'.[6] James went on to become Headmaster of Brigg Grammar School in Lincolnshire and rector of Market Rasen. He married a cousin, Frances, who bore him eighteen children of whom only eight survived to maturity. The eldest boy, Henry, went to Cambridge and became a distinguished academic. Jane met Henry Walter in 1811 while on a visit to her brother Henry in London. On hearing him described as 'the best Classick in the University', she commented 'How such a report would have interested my Father!'.[7] She was surely right in thinking that George Austen would have been proud of his half-brother's grandson. Henry Walter became Professor of Natural Philosophy and Mathematics at the Honourable East India Company College, Haileybury, and demonstrated the breadth of his scholarship by also writing a three-volume *History of England*.

Phylly Walter – a country cousin

The other member of William and Susannah's family who is of particular interest is Philadelphia, known as Phylly. She appears in family biographies in an incidental role, but I am presenting what is known about her in an attempt to do her justice as a person. As the recipient of correspondence from her cousins Eliza and (occasionally) Jane and Cassandra, she played an important, if passive, role in the recording of family events.

As the youngest child of the family, with four elder brothers, Phylly was, not surprisingly, a quiet unadventurous personality. Jane's mother expressed her regret that Phylly did not come and stay more at Steventon, writing in 1786 that Phylly 'might as well be in Jamaica keeping your Brother's House, for anything that we see of you.'[1] We know that she visited Tunbridge Wells together with Mrs Hancock and Eliza in September 1787. Phylly, in a letter to her brother, described the journey in 'an elegant coach and four' and a range of social occasions including a recital by Italian singers, dancing in the Assembly Rooms, a horse race, theatre visits and a dinner party with Francis Motley Austen in Lamberhurst.[2]

Later that year Eliza tried to persuade her cousin to join the Austens for Christmas in Hampshire, where family theatricals were planned, but Phylly was shy, claiming 'I should not have courage to act a part, nor do I wish to attain it'.[3] Phylly also pleaded her domestic duty, to which Eliza replied that 'not leaving your Mother alone is certainly very essential, but would it not be possible to engage some Friend or Neighbour to come and stay with her during so short an absence . . .? I assure You our performance is to be by no means a publick one, since only a selected party of Friends will be present'.[4] But Phylly still refused to join the party and may have gained a reputation in the family for being rather choosy, for in January 1801, Jane Austen wrote to her sister about the latter's account of the festive season with the Knights in Kent: 'Your Christmas gaities are really quite surprising; I think they would satisfy even Miss Walter herself'.[5]

Phylly and Eliza could hardly have been more different, and Phylly was well aware of this. She had none of the Austen wit and could even be said to lack any sense of humour. She also had a tendency, within her own family, to be censorious. When Eliza's mother was dying, Phylly told her brother how she feared that Eliza's misspent youth would catch up with her: 'The gay and dissipated life she has long had so plentiful a share of has not ensur'd her friends among the worthy . . . I always . . . pitied her thoughtlessness. I have frequently . . . regretted the manner of her life . . . she will soon feel the loss and her want of domestic knowledge.'[6] But Phylly had reason to thank Eliza for broadening her horizons, when in April 1788 she made the effort to stay with Eliza in London where they attended the famous trial of the Hancocks' friend Warren Hastings. There she 'had the satisfaction of hearing all the celebrated orators, Sheridan, Burke and Fox.'[7] For one who seldom travelled far, Phylly must have found the experience a stimulating one.

Phylly's correspondence has also given us useful information about the Hampshire branch of the family, one of the very few first-hand descriptions of the novelist herself. In 1788 Jane, then aged twelve and a half, and her family were visiting her great-uncle Francis at The Red House in Sevenoaks. Phylly called on them there and wrote to her brother: 'Yesterday I began an acquaintance with my female cousins, Austens. My uncle, aunt, Cassandra & Jane arrived at Mr F. Austen's the day before. We dined with them there. As it's pure Nature to love ourselves I may be allowed to give the preference to the Eldest [Cassandra] who is generally reckoned a most striking resemblance to me in features, complexion & manners. I never found myself as much disposed to be vain, as I can't help thinking her very pretty . . . The youngest (Jane) is very like her brother Henry, not at all pretty & very prim, unlike a girl of twelve: but it is hasty judgement which you will scold me for. My aunt has lost several fore-teeth, which makes her look old: my uncle is quite white-haired, but looks vastly well: all in high spirits & disposed to be pleased with each other . . . I continue to admire my amiable likeness the best of the two in every respect: she keeps up conversation in a very sensible & pleasing manner. Yesterday they all spent the day with us, & the more I see of Cassandra the more I admire [her] – Jane is whimsical & affected.'8 Perhaps Jane's sharp wit had made Phylly painfully aware of her own lack of humour.

We cannot be sure how much Phylly saw of her Hampshire cousins after that. At least written contact was sustained, for in 1798 Jane wrote a letter of condolence to her cousin on the death of her father William Hampson: 'The loss of so kind & affectionate a Parent, must be a very severe affliction to all his Children, to yourself more especially, as your constant residence with him has given you so much the more constant and intimate Knowledge of his Virtues. – But the very circumstances which at present enhances your loss, must gradually reconcile you to it the better; – the Goodness which made him valuable on Earth, will make him Blessed in Heaven. – This consideration must bring comfort to yourself.'9 Such sensitive wording must have been helpful to the grieving Phylly.

Among Phylly's acquaintances in Tonbridge were some of the Woodgate family. One of them, Mary Anne Humphry, was distantly related to the Austens by marriage. Her paternal uncle was the painter, Ozias Humphry, who may have painted the portrait of old Francis

Austen which is well known among the family portraits. There was considerable intermarriage among people of the same social set, so it is not surprising that a community like Tonbridge should have had so many folk related to each other. Phylly Walter remained a dutiful spinster daughter for over twenty years, until her mother died in 1811. Then, at the advanced age of fifty, she married.

Her husband, George Whitaker, was a mere forty-two. He was the younger son of John Whitaker, a man of learning and for fifty years the highly respected vicar of Pembury, a village four miles south-east of Tonbridge. George was a farmer, a tenant at first, according to Land Tax records, but by the time of his marriage a landowner.[10] The wedding took place at Brisley in Norfolk where the bride's brother Weaver was rector. The Austens were, naturally, delighted at the news. Cousin Cassandra wrote at length: 'I think I cannot give you a better wish, than that you may be as happy as you deserve and that as a Wife you may meet the reward you so well earned as a Daughter. Mr Whitaker will of course feel himself included in every good we desire for you; pray assure him it will give us great pleasure to have an opportunity of being introduced to our new relation, and make our best compts. [compliments] to his Mother and Sister. I shall hope soon to receive from you a very particular account of your new home. From what you have already said I am sure it must be comfortable . . . You are now a Farmer I think and will I trust have the pleasure of seeing your first crop got in in capital order. I quite envy you your Farm, there is so much amusement and so many comforts attending a Farm in the country that those who have once felt the advantages cannot easily forget them . . . Pembury is I suppose in a fine fruit country, I hope you are better off in that respect than we are this year. . .'[11] In another letter the following year, Cassandra expresses her hope for the improved health of Mr Whitaker, who had been unwell with a 'severe fit of gout'.[12]

Without much recorded evidence the picture of Phylly's married life is a sketchy one. George Whitaker's father had died in 1803 and in 1814, when his mother died, there is some indication in the Woodgate correspondence that the family fortunes suffered a setback. Unfortunately the reference is so cryptic that all one can be certain of is that 'circumstances are very much reduced'.[13] By 1827 Cassandra and Phylly were still in contact and material matters were again to the fore, as Cassandra commented: 'I am sorry that Mr W. should have been deprived of any of the goods of this world to which he was entitled, but I am fully convinced that beyond a competence suited to our habits, increase of wealth is not increase of happiness'.[14] As Cassandra had also referred to Phylly's 'tolerably good health' and her 'comfortable home', we can assume the latter's life was not too hard.

In 1833 Cassandra commended Phylly for the 'true Christian philosophy' she had always practised and which Cassandra admired. Phylly still derived 'amusement from needlework' and Mr Whitaker was again unwell.[15] Phylly herself died the following year aged seventy-three, while her husband lived on for another twelve years. In 1840 he seems to have been reasonably prosperous for he owned several houses and an orchard[16] and was sufficiently rich to give the second largest donation (£200) to the village's new church. His and Phylly's memorials can be seen on the wall of Pembury Old Church.

The Sevenoaks Austens – pillars of the community

The town of Sevenoaks is seven miles north of Tonbridge and it was here that Jane Austen came in July 1788 when she stayed with her great-uncle Francis at The Red House, in the High Street. He was an attorney and a notable Sevenoaks figure, trustee of eleven turnpike trusts, Governor of Sevenoaks School, agent for the Knole estate and parliamentary agent for the Duke of Dorset. As befitted his station, he lived in a very elegant house built by Thomas Couchman in 1686, and it was here that he entertained George Austen, with his wife and daughters when they came to stay. The old gentleman, by now aged ninety, was clearly well-disposed towards his nephew George, in whose education he had invested money. During this visit the Walters were invited for a meal where Phylly, as we have already noted, had her first meeting with her cousin the novelist.

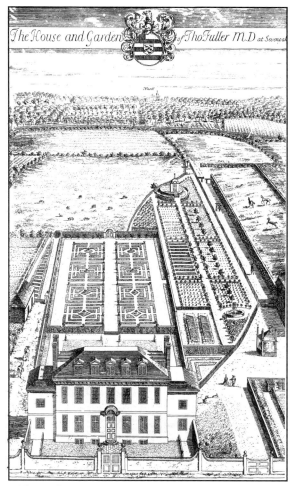

The Red House, Sevenoaks, in 1719, home of Jane's
great-uncle Francis and visited by her in 1788, from
The History of Kent by John Harris. *Sevenoaks Library*

Jane's brother Henry, who had seen the old man a few years
previously, described him thus: 'he wore a wig like a Bishop, & a suit
of light gray ditto, coat, vest & hose. . . he retained a perfect identity
of colour, texture & make to his life's end – I think he was born in
Anne's reign, and was of course a smart man of George the First's. It
is a sort of privilege to have seen and conversed with such a model of
a hundred years since.'[1]

Francis' first wife had been Anne Motley, the wealthy heiress daughter of Thomas Motley, by whom he had one son, Francis Motley, at whose birth Anne died. Francis went on to marry Jane Lennard, widow of Samuel Lennard of West Wickham, who bore him two more sons. According to the novelist's brother she was a 'pleasing amiable woman'.[2] She too was extremely rich and with this marriage Francis acquired extensive property in West Wickham and Orpington, together with the livings of the former and of Chevening, a village five miles north-west of Sevenoaks. Francis's second wife is of interest, as she was the novelist's godmother, though she died before the family visit in 1788.

When his father died in 1791, Francis Motley Austen received a substantial inheritance, which was further augmented on his marriage to another wealthy heiress, Elizabeth Wilson. They lived at Lamberhurst until 1796 when he sold both that property and The Red House, moving to Kippington House on the western outskirts of Sevenoaks, which had been rebuilt in 1760 by Sir Charles Farnaby. Francis Motley was the equivalent in today's money of a multi-millionaire. Although he did not hold anything like the large number of official posts which his father had, he was, like him, a Clerk of the Peace. He had eleven children among whom was John Austen VII, who in 1813 received the living of Chevening.

Jane Austen and Tonbridge

Jane Austen mentions 'Tunbridge' (meaning Tonbridge) in the opening sentence of Sanditon, when she describes the journey taken by Mr and Mrs Parker towards the Sussex coast. But despite the many family links with Tonbridge already described, there is no record of any occasion when she actually visited the town. This does not mean that she did not come to the town, however. It is most likely that any such visit would have been to her father's cousin, Henry, when she was young; written evidence for the early part of her life is patchy. Although Jane may never have visited Tonbridge, she did encounter a number of Tonbridge people in the course of her life. Probably the most well known of these was James Stanier Clarke.

JAMES STANIER CLARKE

Born c.1767 in Minorca, where his father was chaplain to the Governor, James Stanier Clarke came to Tonbridge School c.1778 and proved to be a talented scholar, taking part in the traditional disputations on Skinners' Day (the annual prize-giving) and on that occasion in 1783 reciting a poem of his own composition, 'The Siege of Gibraltar'. He became a naval chaplain and wrote several books on naval themes, including a life of Nelson. While serving on HMS *Impetueux* the captain introduced Clarke to the Prince Regent, who invited him to become his domestic chaplain and librarian.

This appointment enabled Clarke to leave the Navy, and he combined his duties with studying law at Jesus College, Cambridge, eventually gaining his degree in 1816. He relished court life at Brighton and Carlton House and it was through this that he came into contact with Jane. The Prince was an admirer of her novels and Clarke arranged for her to call on him at Carlton House in November 1815. After the visit Jane was invited to dedicate her next novel to His Royal Highness, which she duly did, the work being *Emma*. Clarke then tried to persuade her to write a story with a clergyman as the central character, but she declined, saying she was unequal to the task of portraying a well-educated clergyman's breadth of knowledge. She maintained she was 'the most unlearned & uninformed Female who ever dared to be an Authoress'.[1]

While thanking Jane for the Prince's copy of *Emma*, the irrepressible Revd J.S. Clarke proposed another scheme, a 'Historical Romance, illustrative of the History of the August house of Cobourg'[2] but Jane again refused, saying she 'could no more write a Romance than an Epic Poem'.[3] She later included some of Clarke's ideas in a burlesque *Plan of a Novel*, which circulated within the family.[4] A generous man, Clarke suggested to Jane that she might use his house in Golden Square 'with its Small Library' or his 'Cell at Carlton House' as a 'sort of Half-way House when you come to Town'.[5] He remained a loyal reader of Jane's books and his personal copy of the combined publication *Northanger Abbey* and *Persuasion* survives.[6] Clarke ended his days serving the parish of Tillington, near Petworth, where he died in 1834.[7]

JOHN GEORGE CHILDREN

The second person whom Jane knew of in Tonbridge was John George Children. It is not known if she ever met him, for her only mention of him is a passing reference in a letter to Cassandra in 1796. With

Ferox Hall, home of John George Children, opposite Tonbridge School.

characteristic humour she pokes fun at Children's double Christian names (he, an only child, was named after both his father George and his grandfather John): 'Mr Children's two sons are both going to be married, John & George – . They are to have one wife between them'.[8]

How Jane came to know of the Children family is uncertain but there are several possible connections. When her father was teaching at Tonbridge School, he lived across the road from Ferox Hall, the

Children family home from at least 1755. John George's father, George, had been a pupil at the school from 1750 to 1758, overlapping with George Austen's period as Usher. George Children was an outstanding scholar, who was selected to deliver the Latin speech on Skinners' Day four years running and must certainly have made an impression on Jane's father.

There were also family connections. John George Children's grandfather had married Jane Weller, niece of the redoubtable Elizabeth, the novelist's great-grandmother. And John George's uncle Richard had married Henry Austen's sister-in-law Elizabeth Hooker. Jane may well have heard about these links from her father. She may even have met the Childrens if she ever came to the town, for her father's cousin Henry lived only fifty yards down the road from Ferox Hall.

The Childrens were well-known in Tonbridge where John George's father was a wealthy landowner. They built a laboratory for the study of natural science, which stands at the back of Ferox Hall, now in the form of a cottage. Here they attracted several noted scientists, including Sir Humphry Davy who conducted experiments (some of them dangerous) on the premises. John George became librarian to the Zoology Department of the British Museum. His daughter, Anna Atkins, was a pioneering botanist and photographer and is commemorated by a plaque unveiled at Halstead Place, near Sevenoaks, in 1997.

VICESIMUS KNOX AND THOMAS JEFFERSON – TWO WRITERS
Among the works of literature with which Jane was familiar was an anthology compiled by a Tonbridge School headmaster, Vicesimus Knox. This curiously named individual held the post from 1778 to 1812, following his father who, confusingly, bore the same name. The younger Vicesimus was a scholar and writer, whose *Essays Moral and Literary* received praise from the eminent Dr Johnson. He was known in his lifetime principally for his two anthologies: the first one, *Elegant Extracts, or Useful and Entertaining Passages in Prose, selected for the improvement of Scholars at Classical and other Schools*, was published in 1783 and was recommended by George Austen to his

son Francis as essential reading when he began his life as a sailor in 1788.[9]

The second anthology was of verse: *Elegant Extracts, or Useful and Entertaining Pieces of Poetry, Selected for the Improvement of Young Persons.* It was first published in 1789 and was intended 'to serve as a little Poetical Library, for school-boys, precluding the inconvenience and expence of a multitude of volumes'. This successful work was issued in several editions and became very popular. Jane is known to have had a copy of the *Prose Extracts*, which she gave to her niece, Anna, in 1801 and which survives at the Jane Austen Museum.[10]

Jane mentions *Elegant Extracts* in Chapter IV of *Emma* as the book that the farmer Robert Martin read aloud in the evenings to his mother, sisters and Emma's friend, Harriet Smith. Harriet judged it to be 'very entertaining'.[11] This was probably intended to be the poetry volume since it is referred to again in Chapter IX as containing a verse by Garrick (which in fact it does not).

Another resident of Tonbridge whom Jane knew of was a Mr Jefferson whom she mentions in a letter of 1808. The research of William Jarvis has revealed him to be the Revd Thomas Jefferson, sometime curate of Appledore on the edge of Romney Marsh, who married in 1790 and moved to Tonbridge where he became a schoolmaster.[12] His wife died after bearing five children, and Jefferson remarried. With his second wife he had four more children (one of whom died in infancy). To help pay for the education and upbringing of this large family Jefferson wrote a book, to be published as its title page stated 'solely with the View of assisting the Endeavours of a Parent, who has no professional Preferment, and no other Aid but his Labours in a private school, to support & place out a Family of Eight Children'. Jane Austen, while staying with her brother in Kent, wrote to Cassandra: 'I have read Mr Jefferson's case to Edward [her brother], and he desires to have his name set down for a guinea and his wife's for another . . .'[13] The 'case' is Jefferson's Proposals (or reason) for the publication of his *Two Sermons* and *An Essay Intended as a Vindication of Divine Justice*. Jane later made a request to her sister: 'I wish to have my name put down as a subscriber to Mr Jefferson's works. My Last Letter was closed before it occurred to me how

Title Page of the 1805 edition of *Elegant Extracts or Useful and Entertaining Pieces of Poetry* by Vicesimus Knox, headmaster of Tonbridge School. It shows schoolboys reading and playing cricket. Jane knew this anthology and its companion one of prose extracts. *Tonbridge School Library*

possible, how right & how gratifying such a measure wd. be.'[14] When the book was eventually published it carried a list of 1200 names, of whom 13 were Austens. There were 48 in Southampton where Cassandra was resident and mobilising support on behalf of the cause, which she had probably heard of from old friends in Tonbridge.

The Jefferson family's predicament touched the hearts of Jane and her family. It is satisfying to know that one of Jefferson's sons, Joseph, made a success of his education, becoming a priest and schoolmaster in Jamaica and also that his father lived to the age of seventy-one. The generous subscribers to his book had certainly done well in helping a hard-up Tonbridge family.

JOHN PAPILLON

When Jane Austen arrived in her last home at Chawton in 1809, she encountered as rector there a man who had been the vicar of Tonbridge from 1791 to 1802, John Rawston Papillon. Her local clergyman was therefore from the very place with which her family had so many connections.

Mr Papillon had several links with the Austens. His family came from East Kent and through a seventeenth-century marriage with a member of the Knight family had become distant cousins of the Austens. This connection between the two families became apparent when Thomas Knight died in 1794. In his will he stipulated that John Papillon should receive the living of Chawton when a vacancy next arose, with Jane's brother Henry as the reserve should Papillon refuse it. But John did accept it and Henry remained in the militia. The episode suggests that Jane would at least have known about John Papillon, when he was vicar of Tonbridge. The first thing that John Papillon did when he took over his Hampshire living was to pull down the old vicarage and build a new one but he over-reached himself, for its elaborately designed grounds later had to be modified due to 'too much expence'.[15]

John Papillon was a bachelor and his unmarried state became the subject of a running joke in the Austen circle. In December 1808, when Jane knew she would soon be living in Chawton she wrote to her sister about the notion that the rector there might be an eligible match: 'I am very much obliged to Mrs Knight [cousin of the Austens and widow of the family benefactor] for such a proof of the interest she takes in me – & she may depend upon it, that I *will* marry Mr Papillon, whatever may be his reluctance or my own'.[16] The marriage joke was still running eight years later when Jane wrote to Cassandra: 'I am happy to tell you that Mr Papillon will soon make his offer, probably next Monday as he returns on Saturday'.[17]

Over the years Jane came to know the vicar and his resident sister, Elizabeth, well; she socialised at the vicarage where she met many other people. A letter she wrote in January 1813 testifies to this. Jane was uneasy about her host's demeanour, commenting, 'as usual we wanted a better Master of the House, one less anxious & fidgetty, & more conversible'.[18] Papillon's sister was something of a companion, for Jane shared books from the Chawton Book Society with her, and joined her in walking to the house of a poor family, to whom Elizabeth gave money and Jane gave old clothes.

The link with Papillon was further strengthened in 1817 when Jane's brother Henry became his curate at Chawton. Anticipating his arrival, Jane wrote: 'Our own new Clergyman is expected here very soon, perhaps in time to assist Mr Papillon on Sunday. I shall be very glad when the first hearing is over. It will be a nervous hour for our Pew, though we hear that he acquits himself with as much ease & collectedness, as if he had been used to it all his life.'[19]

Three years later Henry Austen married the rector's niece, Eleanor Jackson.[20] Jane did not live to see this marriage but she knew of Eleanor, whom she mentioned in a letter in 1813 and almost certainly met. Cassandra certainly approved of her, calling her 'an excellent wife' whom Henry wishes would have 'better health'.[21] But Eleanor's health was strong enough to allow her to write her *Epitome of the Old Testament* which was published in 1831. The Papillon connection is one of the many reminders of her family's associations with Tonbridge which Jane Austen received through her reading and correspondence and contact with members of her extended family.

Epilogue

After Jane Austen died in 1817, at the age of forty-one, there was less and less contact between the Hampshire and Kentish branches of the family. There were few reasons to draw members of the Hampshire branch of the family to West Kent, let alone Tonbridge. The last remaining cousin in the area, Phylly Whitaker, continued to correspond with Cassandra and letters from her in reply survive for 1827 and 1832. They indicate that Cassandra visited Godmersham but not what she called, to Phylly, 'your part of the county'.[1] The diaries of her niece, Fanny Knight, by then Lady Knatchbull, endorse this by showing that Cassandra visited her relations in East Kent at two-yearly intervals up to 1833.[2] The only one of Jane's siblings who is recorded as coming to West Kent in his later life is her brother Henry. After becoming a priest in 1816, he served in several parishes in Hampshire until he retired in 1839. With his second wife Eleanor, he then went to live partly in Colchester and partly in Tunbridge Wells. He died of gastritis on 12 March 1850, while living in Tunbridge Wells, and is buried in the old Woodbury Park Cemetery where his gravestone is remarkably well preserved.

To some it may seem surprising that there is so much evidence of the Austen family's links with the Tonbridge area, while at the same time a general lack of awareness among the present population that the Austens had anything to do with the town. Some of their houses survive, several memorials exist, and since September 2000 there is now a plaque to George Austen at Tonbridge School. It is a cause for reflection and also admiration that George Austen and his sister Philadelphia overcame the disadvantage of being orphans, which could have resulted in apathy, rebellion or emotional trauma, but instead led to lives of fulfilment. From his unpromising situation, Jane's father, who was 'blessed with a bright and hopeful disposition',[3] chose to take advantage of every benefit his Tonbridge education could give him, and went on to create with his wife a secure family base for his own offspring. It was a base in which Jane's talents were able to grow and flourish.

In 1802 Vicesimus Knox's son recited a poem at the Annual

Visitation of the School Governors. It was entitled *The Tunbridge School Boy* and spoke of the qualities of one who received a classical education:

polish'd is his ear, and keen
His intellect, he hears, he tastes, he feels,
Till his whole soul elate with ecstasy,
Catching the flame of genius, boldly dares
To emulate the beauty he admires.[4]

Is it too fanciful to suggest that George Austen caught the flame of genius at Tonbridge and passed it to his daughter, Jane?

Bibliography

Andrews, S. M., *Jane Austen. Some aspects of her work, together with her Tonbridge Connections* (Tonbridge, 1949)

Austen-Leigh, R. A., *Austen Papers*, 1704-1856 (London, 1942)

Austen-Leigh, R. A., *Pedigree of Austen* (London, 1940)

Chalklin, C. W. ed., *Georgian Tonbridge* (Tonbridge, 1994)

Collins, I., *Jane Austen and the Clergy* (London, 1994)

Gilson, D. J., *A Bibliography of Jane Austen* (Oxford, 1985); reissued with new Introduction and Corrections (Winchester/New Castle, Delaware, 1997)

Hart, W. G., *The Old School Lists of Tonbridge School* (London, 1933)

Hoole, G. P., *A Tonbridge Miscellany* (Tonbridge, 1985)

Keith-Lucas, B., 'Francis and Francis Motley Austen, Clerks of the Peace for Kent' in Detsicas, A., and Yates, N., eds., *Studies in Modern Kentish History* (Maidstone, 1983)

Lane, M., *Jane Austen's Family through Five Generations* (London, 1984)

Le Faye, D. G., and Austen-Leigh, W. and R. A., *Jane Austen: A Family Record* (London, 1989)

Le Faye, D. G., ed ., *Jane Austen's Letters,* (Oxford, 1995)

Orchard, H. B., *A Look at the Head and the Fifty: A History of Tonbridge School* (London, 1991)

Waldron Smithers, D., *Jane Austen in Kent* (Westerham, 1981)

Tucker, G. H., *A Goodly Heritage: A History of Jane Austen's Family* (Manchester, 1983); reissued as *A History of Jane Austen's Family* (Stroud, Glos., 1998)

Woodgate, G. and G. M., *A History of the Woodgates of Stonewall Park* and of Summerhill in Kent (Wisbech, 1910)

Notes

Introduction
1. Austen-Leigh, R. A., *Austen Papers, 1704-1856* (hereafter *'Austen Papers'*) pp. 132-4

The early Austens
1. Will of John Austen I as referred to in Le Faye, D. G., and Austen-Leigh, W. and R. A., *Jane Austen: A Family Record* (hereafter *'Family Record'*), p.1
2. Tucker, G. H., *A Goodly Heritage*, p.18. Also Gilson, D. J., *A Bibliography of Jane Austen*, p.446
3. Austen-Leigh, R. A., *Pedigree of Austen* (hereafter *'Pedigree'*), p.2

Jane's great-grandmother, Elizabeth Weller – a remarkable woman.
1. Elizabeth's Memorandum and Accounts are reproduced in an abridged form in *Austen Papers*, pp.3-16

Elizabeth Weller's children – in need of education
1. Hoole, G. P., *A Tonbridge Miscellany*, p.75
2. *Pedigree*, p.6
3. *Pedigree*, p.3
4. *Pedigree*, p.5
5. Le Faye, D. G., ed., *Jane Austen's Letters* (hereafter *'Letters'*), No.104, 10-18 August 1814
6. Centre for Kentish Studies, U55 T432
7. *Letters*, No. 51, 20-22 February 1807

Jane's father, George – a handsome man
1. Austen, Jane, *Persuasion*, ed. Chapman, R. W. (Oxford, 1946) p.234
2. Lefroy, Anna, Family History, ms. I am indebted to Alwyn Austen and Deirdre Le Faye for information from this source.
3. Southam, B. C., 'George Austen: Pupil, Usher and Proctor' in the Jane Austen Society *Report* for 2000, pp. 6-11.

George's cousin, Henry – clergyman of West Kent
1. Jarvis, W. A. W., 'The Rev. Thomas Bathurst' in Jane Austen Society *Report* for 1978, pp.8-10. Also parish records research by NADFAS Church Recorders.
2. Letter from Henry T. Austen to James Edward Austen-Leigh, n.d., *Austen Papers*, pp.16-19

3. Letter from Francis W. Austen to Anna Lefroy, 9 October 1855, quoted in *Family Record*, p.45
4. Woodgate, G. and G. M., *A History of the Woodgates of Stonewall Park and of Summerhill in Kent* (hereafter '*Woodgates*'), p.391
5. Butler-Harrison family history quoted in Le Faye, D. and Austen-Leigh, W. and R. A., *A Family Record*, p.79
6. *Letters*, No. 66, 24 January 1809
7. *Woodgates*, p.391
8. *Woodgates*, p.337
9. *Woodgates*, p.309

Jane's Tonbridge aunts – contrasting lives

1. Le Faye, D. G., 'Leonora Austen', in Jane Austen Society *Report* for 1998, pp.55-7
2. Vick, R., 'The Hancocks', in Jane Austen Society *Report* for 1999, pp.19-23
3. *Austen Papers*, p.125
4. Le Faye, D. G., 'Jane Austen and her Hancock Relatives' in *The Review of English Studies* (New Series) Vol. XXX, No. 117, February 1979, pp.12-27

The Austen step relations – the affectionate Walters

1. Hoole, G. P., and Jarvis, W. A. W., 'William Walter' in Jane Austen Society *Report* for 1985, pp.16-18
2. Hoole, G. P., *A Tonbridge Miscellany*, p.79
3. *Austen Papers*, pp.26-7
4. Le Faye, D. G., 'Three Austen Family Letters' in *Notes and Queries*, September 1985, pp.329-35
5. *Austen Papers*, pp.88-92
6. *Austen Papers*, pp.99-105
7. *Letters*, No. 78, 24 January 1813

Phylly Walter – a country cousin

1. Le Faye, D. G., 'Three Austen Family Letters' in *Notes and Queries*, September 1985, p.329-35
2. *Austen Papers*, pp.124-5
3. *Austen Papers*, pp.123-6
4. *Austen Papers*, pp.128-9
5. *Letters*, No. 29, 3-5 January 1801
6. *Austen Papers*, pp.143-9

7. *Austen Papers*, pp.129-30
8. *Austen Papers*, pp.130-1
9. *Letters*, No. 8, 8 April 1798
10. Centre for Kentish Studies, Land Tax Records 1806 and 1810
11. *Austen Papers*, pp.248-9
12. *Austen Papers*, pp.250-3
13. *Woodgates*, pp.190-1
14. *Austen Papers*, pp.274-7
15. *Austen Papers*, pp.287-9
16. Tithe Map Apportionment 1839-41, Centre for Kentish Studies R29/17

The Sevenoaks Austens – pillars of the community
1. *Austen Papers*, pp.16-19
2. *Ibid.*

Jane Austen and Tonbridge
1. *Letters*, No. 132(D), 11 December 1815
2. *Letters*, No. 138(A), 27 March 1816
3. *Letters*, No. 138(D), 1 April 1816
4. Austen, Jane, *Minor Works*, ed. Chapman, R. W. (Oxford, 1972) pp.428-30
5. *Letters*, No. 132(A), 21 December 1815
6. Gilson, D. J., 'Jane Austen and James Stanier Clarke' in *The Book Collector*, No. 27, 1978, pp.109-10. Clarke's copy is now in King's College Library, Cambridge.
7. Viveash, C., 'Jane Austen – The Divine and the Donkey' in *Persuasions*, No. 16, 1994, pp.16-20
8. *Letters*, No. 6, 15-16 September 1796
9. Collins, I., in Appendix 1 of B.C. Southam's *Jane Austen and the Navy* (London, 2000)
10. Le Faye, D. G., 'New Marginalia in Jane Austen's Books' in *The Book Collector*, No. 49, 2000, pp.222-6
11. Austen, Jane, *Emma*, ed. Chapman, R. W. (Oxford, 1966) p.29
12. Jarvis, W. A. W., 'Mr Jefferson's Case' in Jane Austen Society *Report* for 1989, pp.15-18
13. *Letters*, No. 52, 15-17 June 1808
14. *Letters*, No. 54, 26 June 1808
15. Kaplan, D., 'Henry Austen and John Rawston Papillon' in Jane Austen Society *Report* for 1987, pp.11-15
16. *Letters*, No. 62, 9 December 1808

17. *Letters*, No. 146, 16-17 December 1816
18. *Letters*, No. 78, 24 January 1813
19. *Letters*, No. 150(C) 24 January 1817
20. Midgley, W., 'The Revd Henry and Mrs Eleanor Austen' in Jane Austen Society *Report* for 1978, pp.14-19
21. *Austen Papers*, pp.284-5

Epilogue
1. *Austen Papers*, pp.274-7
2. Fanny Knight's diaries are in the Knatchbull Family Archives at the Centre for Kentish Studies, Maidstone, catalogue mark U951 F24.
3. Lefroy, Anna, Family History, ms.
4. Knox, V., *Elegant Extracts: or Useful and Entertaining Pieces of Poetry* (London, 1809)

THE AUSTENS OF WEST KENT

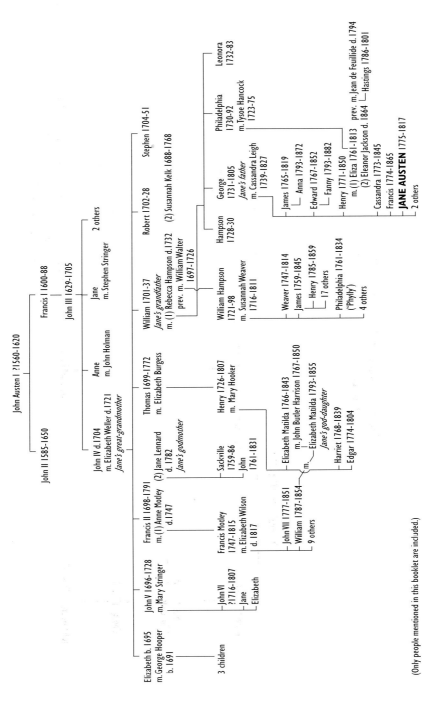

(Only people mentioned in this booklet are included.)

THE CONNECTION BETWEEN THE AUSTEN FAMILY
AND THE CHILDREN AND KNIGHT FAMILIES

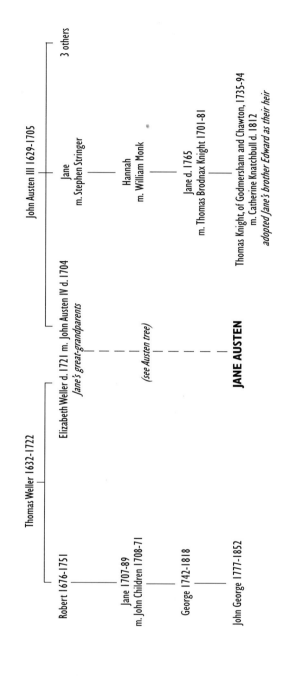

John Austen III 1629-1705

Thomas Weller 1632-1722

Elizabeth Weller d. 1721 m. John Austen IV d. 1704
Jane's great-grandparents

Jane
m. Stephen Stringer

3 others

Robert 1676-1751

Jane 1707-89
m. John Children 1708-71

(see Austen tree)

Hannah
m. William Monk

George 1742-1818

Jane d. 1765
m. Thomas Brodnax Knight 1701-81

John George 1777-1852

JANE AUSTEN

Thomas Knight, of Godmersham and Chawton, 1735-94
m. Catherine Knatchbull d. 1812
adopted Jane's brother Edward as their heir

Index

Allnutt, Francis (née Woodgate) 27
Atkins, Jane *see* Austen
Austen
    Anne (née Motley) 40
    Cassandra (née Leigh), Jane's mother 24, 32, 36
    Cassandra, Jane's sister 12, 34, 36, 37, 38, 42, 44, 46, 47, 48
    Edgar Francis 22, 24, 26, 27
    Edward *see* Knight
    Eleanor (née Jackson) 31, 47, 48
    Elizabeth (née Burgess) 17
    Elizabeth (née Weller), Jane's great-grandmother 13-20, 43
    Elizabeth (née Wilson) 40
    Elizabeth, daughter of John V 20
    Elizabeth Matilda *see* Butler Harrison
    Francis I 11
    Francis II 9, 16, 20, 21, 24, 36, 38-40
    Francis, Jane's brother 26-27, 44
    Francis Motley 20, 22, 24, 35, 40
    George, Jane's father 17, 20-24, 25, 29-34 *passim*, 38, 43, 48, 49
    Hampson 17
    Harriet 26, 27-28
    Henry, George's cousin 17, 22, 24-28, 32, 40, 43
    Henry, Jane's brother 29, 31, 36, 39, 46, 47, 48
    Jane (née Atkins) 12
    Jane, daughter of John V 20
    Jane, the novelist 9-12, 15, 17, 20, 24, 26, 27, 29-31, 34-36, 38-39, 40-49
    Jane (formerly Lennard) 40
    Jane *see* Stringer
    Joan, wife of John I 11
    John I 10, 11
    John III 12-15
    John IV 13-15
    John V 16, 19-20, 23
    John VI 20
    John VII 40
    Leonora 17, 29
    Mary (née Hooker) 26
    Mary (née Stringer) 20
    Philadelphia *see* Hancock
    Rebecca (née Hampson, later Walter), Jane's grandmother 17, 31
    Robert 19
    Stephen 19, 21, 29
    Susannah (née Kelk) 17, 19, 21
    Thomas 17, 25
    William, Jane's grandfather 14, 17-19, 31

Blair House 17
Bordyke 13
Broadford 10, 11, 13, 15, 20, 23
Brodnax, Thomas *see* Knight
Butler Harrison
    Elizabeth Matilda (née Austen) 26-28
    Elizabeth Matilda, daughter of above 27
    John 27

Cambridge 20, 25, 33, 34, 41
Canterbury 12
Carlton House 41
Cawthorn, Revd James 22-23
Chauntlers 13
Chawton 10, 12, 27, 46, 47
Chevening 10, 40
Chiddingstone 25
Children
    Elizabeth (née Hooker) 43
    George 42-43
    John 42-43
    John George 10, 42-43
    Richard 43
Clarke, Revd James Stanier 9, 41-42
Cranbrook 10

Davy, Sir Humphry 43
Dorset, 3rd Duke of 38

Fenton, Elijah 16
Ferox Hall 10, 42-43
Feuillide
    Eliza de (née Hancock, later Austen) 10, 29-31, 32-35 *passim*
    Hastings de 31
    Jean François Capot de 30
Fosse Bank 26, 28

Gloucester 17, 31
Godmersham 12, 48
Goudhurst 10, 12
Grovehurst 11

Hampson
    Sir George 17, 31
    Rebecca *see* Austen

Hancock
  Eliza *see* Feuillide
  Philadelphia (née Austen) 17, 29-31, 34
  Tysoe 29-30
Hastings, Warren 30, 35
Holman, John 15, 20
Hooker
  Elizabeth *see* Children
  Mary *see* Austen
Hooper
  Elizabeth ('Betty', née Austen) 16, 21
  George 16
Horsmonden 10-12, 19, 20
Humphry
  Mary Anne 36
  Ozias 36

Ightham 32, 33

Jackson, Eleanor *see* Austen
Jefferson, Revd Thomas 43-46

Kelk, Susannah *see* Austen
Kippington House 40
Knight
  Edward (formerly Austen), Jane's
    brother 12, 44
  Fanny (formerly Austen), Jane's niece 48
  Jane (née Monk) 12
  Thomas (formerly Brodnax) 12
  Thomas, son of above 46
Knox, Vicesimus 43-45, 48

Lamberhurst 35, 40
Lefroy, Anna (née Austen), Jane's niece 19, 44
Leigh, Cassandra *see* Austen
Lennard
  Jane *see* Austen
  Samuel 40
Lyons *see* Powells

Maidstone 32
Motley
  Anne *see* Austen
  Thomas 40

Orpington 40
Oxford 23-24, 25

Papillon
  Revd John 10, 46-47
  Elizabeth 47
Parsonage, The 32
Pembury 37-38
Powells 16

Prince Regent, The 9, 41-42
Priory, The 13

Red House, The
  (Sevenoaks) 9, 36, 38-39, 40
  (Tonbridge) 13

Seal 32
Sevenoaks 9, 21, 25, 33, 36, 38-40, 43
  School 15-17, 19, 20, 38
Shipbourne 24, 25, 32
Southampton 27, 28, 46
Spencer, Revd Richard 22
Steventon 12, 24, 25, 30, 32, 34
Stringer
  Jane (née Austen) 12
  Stephen 12, 15, 20

Tonbridge
  Parish Church 9, 13, 18, 19, 22, 23, 25, 28
  School 9, 16, 20, 21-25, 26, 27, 30, 31,
    33, 41, 42-45, 48-49
Tunbridge Wells 10, 34, 48

Walter
  Henry 34
  James 33-34
  Philadelphia ('Phylly') *see* Whitaker
  Rebecca (née Hampson) *see* Austen
  Susannah (née Weaver) 32, 37
  Weaver 37
  William 17, 31
  William Hampson 24, 31-33, 34, 36
Weaver, Susannah *see* Walter
Weller
  Elizabeth *see* Austen
  Jane 43
  Robert 13
  Thomas 13
West Wickham 25, 26, 40
Whitaker
  George 37-38
  Revd John 37
  Philadelphia ('Phylly', née Walter) 32,
    33-38, 48
Wilson, Elizabeth *see* Austen
Woodbury Park Cemetery 48
Woodgate
  Anne 27
  Frances *see* Allnutt
  Maria 27
  Sarah 27

Yalding 10